ONE MAN
TWO EXECUTIONS

Arjun Rajendran is the author of *Snake Wine* (Les Éditions du Zaporogue, 2014), *The Cosmonaut in Hergé's Rocket* (Paperwall, 2017) and a chapbook, *Your Baby Is Starving* (Aainanagar/VAYAVYA, 2017). Arjun was the Charles Wallace Fellow in Creative Writing (University of Stirling, Scotland, 2018). He was also the former poetry editor at *The Bombay Literary Magazine* and the founder of The Quarantine Train, a poetry community that is a response to the great pandemic.

ONE MAN
TWO
EXECUTIONS

ARJUN
RAJENDRAN

First published in hardback in 2020 by Context, an imprint of
Westland Publications Private Limited

Published in paperback in 2023 by Context, an imprint of
Westland Books, a division of Nasadiya Technologies Private Limited

No.269/2B, First Floor, 'Irai Arul', Vimalraj Street, Nethaji Nagar,
Alapakkam Main Road, Maduravoyal, Chennai 600095

Westland, the Westland logo, Context and the Context logo are the
trademarks of Nasadiya Technologies Private Limited, or its affiliates.

Copyright © Arjun Rajendran, 2020

ISBN: 9789357765718

10 9 8 7 6 5 4 3 2 1

The views and opinions expressed in this work are the author's own and
the facts are as reported by him, and the publisher is in no way liable for
the same.

All rights reserved

Typeset by Jojy Philip, New Delhi 110 015
Printed at Saurabh Printers Pvt. Ltd.

No part of this book may be reproduced, or stored in a retrieval system,
or transmitted in any form or by any means, electronic, mechanical,
photocopying, recording, or otherwise, without express written
permission of the publisher.

For my father,
who is always mending my sails

Acknowledgements

There are many individuals and organisations I wish to highlight, and whose support has nourished my work over the years. My family, above all, for treating me with kid-gloves, and always doing the best they can in their old age, and to Misha, our dog.

I also wish to express my immense gratitude to my fellowship advisor, Gemma Robinson, the faculty members at the University of Stirling and the former secretary of the Charles Wallace India Trust (CWIT), Richard Alford, for recognising the worth of my historical project. I thank Dinesh Prasad and his family for hosting me, so generously, in London so that I could take my research to the National Maritime Museum in Greenwich.

Thanks also to the descendants of the diarist, Ananda Ranga Pillai, who, one evening in Pondicherry, opened the doors of their illustrious ancestor just for me.

I cannot thank my agent Kanishka Gupta enough, for his relentless faith in this collection, and the poetry editor at Westland, Karthik Venkatesh, for giving these poems a reputed home.

To all my friends, and to Nidhi, for inspiring every poem in the 'Peapod' series.

The poems in this collection have appeared in the following magazines/periodicals:

Santa Clara
Sacramento
Dubai
Ice Storm | *Coldnoon*, October 2017

Begum in a Counting House
Rise, and begone to thy house!
Chéseaux's Comet
Marie Gertrude
The Dûbash's Gift
Epistle
The Storm | *DOMUS India,* June 2018

Lubbay | *Madras Courier*, May 2018

Who Rings the Doorbell?
Carousel | *Indian Quarterly*, Monsoon 2018

Were It Not For | *The Gollancz Book of South Asian Science Fiction*, 2018

Appointment Mirza	*Manalveedu*, 2018
Why Aliens Shun India	*Star*Line*, 2018
Who Buys From the Slave Dealer	*Pratik, 2019*
The Dog-Catcher One Man: Two Executions	*Saaranga Magazine, 2019*
Six Poems—The Girl in the Peapod	*Saaranga Magazine, 2020*
Delhi, Texas	*Helter Skelter*, Volume 7
Four Poems	*The Alipore Post*, June 2020
Four Poems	*The Extinction Violin*, 2021

Contents

I
Pondichéry

Historical Notes	3
Execution of a Deserter	5
Lunar Eclipse	6
Begum in a Counting House	7
Who Buys From the Slave Dealer	8
Rise, and begone to thy house!	9
Chéseaux's Comet	10
Marie Gertrude	11
The Dûbash's Gift	12
Epistle	13
Coja Petrus Uscan	14
The Storm	15
Durian	16
Desecration	17
Lubbay	18
The Influence of Saturn	19
Cafre	21
The Dancing-Girl	22
The Fiddler's Suicide	23

The Dog-Catcher	25
One man: Two executions	26
~~Ç Ç Ç Ç~~	27
Where the English Encamped	28
Dovecote	29
Destruction	30
Lorenzo	31
The Last Cédille	32
Campanology	33
The Pirates of Malabar	35
Smuggling the Dacoit	36
guzzerati girl, riverbank	38
The Lascar's Wish	40
Pirate	42

II
The Girl in the Peapod

Tsuru no Ongaeshi	45
Movie Date	47
When you Travel	49
Sketch of you reading my favourite childhood book	50
Watercolour	51
Loving your Poem	53
Publishing	55
Editing You	56
Burning Question	58

Molly	59
Can't	61
The Girl in the Peapod	62
My Glasses are Foggy Again	63
Of an Alien Moon	64
Accro	65
The Golden Aureole	66
Hff	68
I don't do gifts	70
Confessing in the Library	72
T minus N	74
Standard Candle	77
Get a Room	79
Will You Be There	82
Envelop	85
To Salt	87
Insecurity	90

III
Were It Not For

Not You	93
Ice Storm	94
Disgrace	95
Don't Ring the Doorbell	96
Carousel	97
Ferris Wheel	99

Park Train	100
Appointment	101
ELISA	102
Mirza	104
Were It Not For	105
Santa Clara	107
Sacramento	108
Dubai	109
playing truant	110
My old man's photograph on Sartre's tomb	111
Postcard from Stirling	116
Butterfly Calendar	118
Passport	119
How They Went	120
Why aliens shun India	121
Delhi, Texas	122
Editing	124

I
Pondichéry

Historical Notes

The poems in this section, spanning the years between 1739 and 1749, are set in French colonial Pondicherry/Pondichéry, during the Carnatic wars.

The decades preceding the famous Battle of Plassey (1757), where the English won their victory over the Nawab of Bengal, were tumultuous. Several potentates, royals and colonial powers: the Danish, the Portuguese, the English, the French, the Mughals and the Marathas sought to establish their dominions along the Coromandel coast.

The research that went into these historical poems, owes a debt to the diaries of Ananda Ranga Pillai (1709–61), a meticulous diarist, and a dûbash (interpreter) to the French governor, François Dupleix.

Originally written in Tamil, the diaries haven been translated, by numerous colonial historians interested in this oft-overlooked time, into English and the archives are freely available at several online resources. This book largely profits from the anecdotes, footnotes and chronicles of caste, astrology and maritime records drawn from Volumes One to Six of Pillai's twelve diaries.

While some of the incidents described can be sourced to the diaries, enormous liberty has been taken to release facts and apocrypha into the realm of the imagination, to re-create the interiorities of the populace of a town during war-time.

Execution of a Deserter

1738

From the bow of the St. Géran, a boatswain
catches the glint of muskets

The masts concur: land is a macabre notion
that's approaching fast

A ditch yonder fills with the soldier's fear—
anyone watching from the ship

smells it in the hull, sees bales of broadcloth
reddening around the helmsman

The blindfold is also an eyewitness; it lies not
far from the soil where he last knelt

Sixteen gun salutes from the fort's ramparts
erase the southern burial

Lunar Eclipse

20th July / ஆடி, 1739

Near the anchorage, the sightless ruminate among themselves,
determine the eclipse is like a hole in their remembrance

The governess in her marjoram gown lifts her gaze heavenward;
nine-tenths of the surface area is shadowed from her window

In the basilica's stained glass, acolytes are celestially extinguished
Doppelgängers congregate on pews meant for the left-hand caste

Begum in a Counting House

3rd June/வைகாசி, 1740

Next to accounts of *doucers*, bills of lading
and mouseholes, the begum rests, inflammable.

The men who do the accounting have left
for the day. When she begins cooking, it's too

late to douse her. To explain to the Imâm Sâhib,
who cannot reconcile how a hookah

could steal his wife. Not a malady, or a colonist
harbouring a taste for pretty *moosulmans*

hidden by palanquins, decorum—just coals, angrier
than the eyes of an invader from Isfahan who

couldn't bear to see another's title on the coinage.
If metal can forget its loyalties, if the name

preceding a Shah can overnight change
from Muhammad to Nãdir, then why doubt

fire will overreach God's will; make ash
of Chinese *lampas*, or hesitate burning innocence?

Who Buys From the Slave Dealer

1743

The lascar whipped fifty times for stealing pepper,
laments the sea to his lover; *they* branded

thieves with the figure of a dog—she hears it growl
in his palm, feels its tongue upon her nape, her chest.

A fortnight after, a fettered slave-dealer curses his
luck. It had always worked: the magic paint, betel

and nut were potent; quietened their tongues
long enough to shave their heads, to chain a leg

and clothe them in black. The Frenchman paid him
well, made a fortune smuggling locals to Mascareigne.

This colonist now sent home with a dismissal—naughty
boy on his return voyage muttering *quel dommage!*

Rise, and begone to thy house!

In the Church of Capuchins, 1745

At the altar, she kneels
before the priest in her muslin robe,
unaware that Hungary water is
       intertwining its scent with holy water

Pinching his nose, his cane invades her hair-knot,
shatters her prayer—its Tamil
phonemes throbbing
       about his feet in butchered defeat

*Art thou not
a married woman? Art thou a dancing woman?*

Through her humiliation, her focus is lambent
on the thorny crown

The priest shaming her
husband, disrobing her with words in this land
where another god sartorially saves honour

Chéseaux's Comet

1744

Flanked by cymbalists, soldiers on Acheen horses
& led by an elite of the company, the palanquin

moved towards the governor's palace with the great
comet. More than the radiance of any potentate—

nawab, Mahratta, or Queen—this celestial messenger
seen across continents, in the spyglasses of pirates

& admirals, leaned its nucleus against the coastal
hearts of left-hand castes, against the cold ribs

of a lascar's widow, or Lubbays. Ignoring gifts of silk,
pagodas (8½ touches thick) and nautch girls, it resumed

its voyage, its sextuple tail aiming auguries at
the governess, yet to outlive her daughter and grandchild.

Marie Gertrude

1746

ponies, pearls, saltpeter, sailors
doubloon
incense
coral
fowl
tea

: but war also steals names

> *Marie*, who became (*Khizr*)
> *Mîr*

is now not as much frigate or fluyt
as fish—so her sails calmly dream,
so admirals in their ships, overlook
her not being English,
and salt salts
secret

The Dûbash's Gift

1738

Mascareigne, Mozambique, Tenasserim, Mocha,
their lavish inventories, the fort booming

gun-salutes for merchant vessels, nawâb, governor
equines from Acheen and arecanut gains:

all these, and more, fade the moment he realises
why his reflection doesn't know him anymore,

and immortality brings him to laughter—a portrait
commissioned by a trader he saved from ruin

now stands in place of the mirror, catching his
heartbeat, mustachio, earrings and ego, by surprise

Epistle

From Jeanne Dupleix, 1746

Behind the letter to Mahfuz Khân—berserk by the looting
of Fort St. George—is a governess, Christian. But mainly a mollusk

rarer than a reverse spiralled conch—a woman who can write.
The mace-bearer sent with portraits and china plates to appease

the warrior, also carries the epistle: intended as sister to brother,
a gamble of intention against etiquette, words aimed to arrest

flintlocks, assuage ransack before Muhammadans battle the flag,
before cannon balls punish fort walls with slaughter; and the bereaved

knock on taverns, tombstones, hulls: for peace, never pleasure.
Outside a tent on the Ariyankuppam's banks, horses steal sleep.

Inside, a silhouette burning a seal releases ambergris—he reads
his only letter from a woman, its sisterly plea. A candle underneath.

Coja Petrus Uscan

Madras, 1746

Under his roof, though the monsieur knows
Uscan's loyalties lie with the British

But the Armenian doesn't distinguish him from
his enemy—building the Marmalong

has perhaps taught him not to burn bridges
Why worry about the flag of the ship

as long as it will carry his heart for burial in Julfa?
It's owing to this he will never confess

his real thoughts to his guest, whose soldiers strip
Fort St. George like a native mistress

The Storm

1746

The townsfolk think the sky is hurt
because a fort was plundered

Winds the speed of the governor's
fury snap rigging, topple masts

Anchored in his disbelief is the ship,
Subterfuge; its supercargo, betrayal

The governess— her ear to his heart—
perceives the eye of the storm, christens

it *La Bourdonnais;* after the admiral
charting her husband's disgrace

Durian

1746

Which ill-wind brought the ship to Pondichéry,
twenty durians in its hold?

The package, opened in the governor's house,
prompts ancestors in portraits

to clench their noses; a fruit reaching across
death, killing their inability

to smell or rest behind painted oil for centuries
with red grapes and globes

Through windows, the durians attack natives,
the fort, and enemy sepoys

by the river, routing them
—muskets abandoned—till Chandernagore

Desecration

1747

No priest in the Iswaran temple will clean the filth hurled
from St. Paul's church

Luminous, the governess dines on china and desecration
They arrive: children,

and their children, to scoop shards, stool, eyes never meeting
the worshippers' who,

unable to decide the worser of the two sins, curse the evening's
evil, astrological stars

Lubbay

Kâlâpettâi, 1746

Nearly dawn, the fisherfolk already at sea
Everything falls into something's net
Following its nose, a jackal scents flesh,

situates corruption with urgent stealth
Carrion wetting its jawline—tendons, brooch,
buttons, poniard gashes and pus

A turban under the moss stripped of jewels
Scabbard, sockets, gut, dignity: vacated
hind-legs scratching out ringless toes

Minus one follower: unless the Imâm counts
this beast, sniffing, licking femur tearing
through silk, leaving paw-prints in sunrise

The Influence of Saturn

July, 1747

The dûbash fluent in Tamil and French.
Pondichéry's many castes, mourning:
every vase to its withering.

His twelve volumes on battles, commerce,
courtesans, ships and shipments,
curd-rice, arecanut godowns,

espionage and storms debilitating.
Or the sly governess,
her blaspheming, her calumny

to his master—her second husband,
not that *it* should matter.
His thirteenth volume: addressing

Saturn—*pourquoi? yein?*
pourquoi? yein? pourquoi? ye…
Just before the marriage, choking

his daughter with its planetary ring.
Unwritten, but here divined:
the thirteenth's footnote about the bridegroom

nameless, his astrological blood seeking
just one vengeance for satur-
    nine.

Cafre

1747

It's propitious when a matchlockman's palm
homes an enemy ear; that the rest

of him escaped is (counterintuitively) fortunate
Colombo arrack for this cafre enslaved

in Mombasa, and now, the company's chattel—
but surely the trophy deserves more: a lactating

Negress or Tamil for the soldier, to suckle a memory
before shackles, cargo-holds and his first

sunrise illuminating Pondichéry like a new
word acquired in a delirium made of snake-bite

The Dancing-Girl

1747

The hare crossing Bangâru's path to Pondichéry
doesn't compel her to return.

In the palace, candle-light from a chandelier
laces her remembrance with hautboys.
Staring into the governess' eyes, she

anticipates the bribe expected to recompense
her for the Batavia arrack the soldiers seized
from her farm. She doesn't plead:

*you are a rich woman, madame, and I,
a moor's dancing-girl…*

Instead, she hurls her contempt
at the Frenchwoman's offer, and exits—
neither precisely eminent, nor exactly a pauper.

The Fiddler's Suicide

1747

Blossoms lining an old throat-
incision;
her body, levitating
        since sundown—
resisting every shaman and priest.
The lowly fiddler, inspired by Neptune,
began a tune for his beloved:
first breaking the chandelier's
crystal hearts,
        then toppling the grandfather clock
        made from coffin wood.
She, still above her four poster-bed,
        reciting couplets
in tongues Persian and Hindoostani—
a sweet *afim.*
The cordage
in the *St. Geran*'s model
snapping
like sin, the fiddler's violin
playing by itself
        the music of their kisses beneath
the damaged

lighthouse (before she
returned in deceit to her spouse).
    *Please let me love… you've just
made me fly but it can't*

                    be

    just you.
That he had no idea of passion
this high or haunting.
They found him atop
a hatching sea turtle,
the fiddle's string traversing
his temple.

The Dog-Catcher

1747

Gumastas, sowcars, spies and mahouts
maybe important—but then
there is Savari, the dog-catcher, searching

near the town gates, in kilns, the riverbank:
for canines to drown
so his only playmate, the Topass who

spasmed seeing water, and recoiled
from sunlight, returns wearing the sukkûpachi
beads he was buried in

These murders might matter: the governess's
son in Junkceylon, the Imâm's Lubbay;
yet nothing haunts Savari like monsieur B's

strange tale of the 2500 Dutchmen killed
by 600 dogs—their howls shipped
from Europe, their fathomless avoirdupois

One man: Two executions

1748

When divinity spoke through
a broken noose,
       and *Clemency*—the name
  of the schooner—
brushed its masts inside
spectators, when a rope's
    courage failed
 to end this man skeletal
      with voyage, rats, rancid
port mistresses;
the priest
(foaming against custom)
condemned
        the condemned
  soul to a second hanging,
      his epitaph,
     a ~~palimpsest~~
And to the officer prepared
to free the almost-hung: *it's holier*
   than silence, this ignoring
a lord who absolves
     thick-necked vermin

1748

Sunrise, painted cloths, a mid-wife
in a weaver's street pulls out
—*in disbelief*—four
    babies from a vernacular womb

Natives and Europeans alike behold
these Tamil tadpoles: maiden
    navigations devoured
        by ~ sea-monsters ~

Soon, the loyal siblings join
their still-born firsts, and the gravedigger,
    indifferent but purposed,
inters the Coromandel quadruplets

But the mere sight of the French army,
O mother, is said to make the pregnant miscarry
    And in her insomnia, the cavalry's hoofs
exhume her nameless dead

Where the English Encamped

1748

The hookah that burnt down the counting house
              wasn't an arsonist; *that* fire wasn't
translation's child.

              But war clouds now blow
over from the French into Tamil,
      from the governor's lips into the peons'
 palms—each coin,

a face lit by the smouldering
huts of Muhamaddans who will not stop counting
the irrevocable.

      Each coin,
a warning for the poor to never harbour the enemies
of Louis XV.

Dovecote

1748

Hiding among eggshells,
near sunlight filtering
through droppings-stained
windows

As the shelling
(English) threatened to pluck
the dovecote,
feathers might have seemed

Like ships devoured by the sea—
only strips of wood
branching from a spine
that's unseen light

Then a silence allows them
to see a child's head
in a nest, waiting to be hatched
by enemy fire

Fashioning a needle from a beak,
a Topass stitches
prayer into the morning's
pieces

Destruction

1748

Not the shelling but muscles that ripped out the doors.
Not the English, but Father Coeurdoux,

who clocked—in his blows—fifty years
of inability to hammer and spit at the idols.

Not enemy soldiers but converts and coffers who split
Vishnu in the middle, and kicked devotees

trying to save *vâhanams* on shoulder-poles.
No military excuse like *a watch-tower needs*

the spot more than god. Just the cowardly Tamils,
who couldn't learn from the Muhamaddans

whose ancient mosque (though similarly condemned),
still lies to the west of St. Paul's church.

Lorenzo

1748

Six half-caste boys fetched by the Governor
from Bengal—only Lorenzo was

a musician (*though music cannot seduce shots*)
Seeing the short-Maratha Nâyakkan's head

fallen to a cannon from Rear-Admiral
Boscawen's end, his nerves were riddled

with the flute-holes of war, his melodies
drowned in the cross-fire between batteries

A thigh lay hemorrhaging against Pondichéry's
cheek—the bone sticking out, tuned to agony

That none could save this low-born, the favourite
of the man arrogant in his skeletal masterplan

The Last Cédille

1748, 28th of March

The eaglewood unloaded
from Mijnheer Tempezehl's galleon:
its perfume, a promise
that never existed in Tamil.

The boatswain hands *him* a palmyra-leaf
letter: *her* fishhooks— *ça va,*
        irremplaçable,
                soupçon…

Then *préçieux* (its c, skewed
    punitively;
    baiting his saturnine sleep)

Arming the last cédille in his flintlock,
                (je suis fier de toi…‖ பெருமை)
the English come under aim; under their wigs,
the source, it seems, of all his misery—
but if only blowing their brains
could touch her across the centuries.

Campanology

18th century, 28th of March

Their tryst is arranged
through the church bell's peals

Five rings (a snake's five gems)
when it's moonless

means safe to meet
If not refuged by a marooned

keel, they clandestine in his study:
sin within incunabula,

the Hungary water
on her skin, his tongue an oar

moisturizing her bioluminescent
moles, from wrist, to the trench

fathomless, a ladybug nebula
their intimacy telescopes

*arrête, arrête! entends la cloche!
Mais mon amour,* all this Latin

thirsts to be explored…
And why return to scurvy,

to an eclipsed matrimony
during the weakening siege!

Synchronized with heartbeats,
their bellicose appeals

The Pirates of Malabar

1747

Along the waters
of Anjengo and Tellicherry,
           Angrias in their gallivats attack
from the stern.

Their late pirate lord, Conajee,
his one illegitimate son blinding
      the other—*at least your lungs,*
brother, may enjoy the mizzenmasts embers.

           Near Bombay, Portuguese
powers waning; and the French Téméraire,
Jupiter—its forty guns and 400 slaves,
falls to the son legitimate.

Dutch, Danish, Portuguese, English, Mahratta.
A moribund sultanate
whose nawabs write to the governor
      to restore broken mechanical-dolls.

A bomb ketch orbits *Jupiter* like a moon.
      In the galleys, coffers breathing
each others' destinies can't sleep
      on the ship's demonizing gravity.

Smuggling the Dacoit

1748, 28th of March

The *kallar* bought
for six rupees by the governess,

flees behind a diver's
daughter—in the visible side

of her ambergris face, he confabulates
a once ardour in a guineaman.

They pass gallows where slaves
hung like lanterns autopsic.

She grips—gazing straight—his branded
wrist: *don't falter, these ghosts don't matter*.

The sudden aroma of elephant-foot
from a shack's conjee

almost salivates him from escape.
His stealth shivers in the knowledge

of the moment, imminent
with sorrow. While being smuggled

to Mahé, her risk swells in his throat,
a tempest. That the only part

of him never enslaved, throbs
in her potential mistake. Divers

in their masulas, unaware. Her
palimpsest touch; his lovelorn wrist.

guzzerati girl, riverbank

– 18th century, March 28, Arayankuppam

A colony of funnels
by the riverbank
is where dragonflies hatch.

From here, their resplendence mocks
flags on merchant vessels.

She, who's never flown
to an unknown street,
drops an ant into a cone,
feels herself
sucked
inside its mouth as the larva
clams its pincers
upon the diminutive-red-worker.

Long after the sand settles,
a Tamil boy—only witness to her experiment—
peeking through an anchor's gap,
feels four wings in place
of his brown limbs.

He flutters near her throat—
an āytam (ஃ) in inverse:
necromantic, tribal.

The Lascar's Wish

28th March

I see her on the top-mast,
leeward, exposing a *nautical*
cleavage.

The captain of the *Kraken*
suspects I have dorsal fins.
That I pilfer his opium.

There is no avoiding
the reefs: '*le naufrage
        est proche
        mon amour*!'

But the sea-breeze moves
under her tongue,
speaks a tongue that illiterates

this lascar.
When she descends, the rum
on my breath

will scuttle her
marriage.
Harnessed to flying fish,

we avoid the *Kraken*'s broadside;
hoping the eye of the *orage*
shall grant my wish.

Pirate

your eyes had vanished inside
their sockets…
my mouth on your right-breast
      like a cobra's around an egg
when I heard you mutter
pirate, pirate
in sweet kidnap, sadism
your breath ripping away the topmast,
its skull and crossbones burying
          us under savagery
in your fictitious island where
I am free to
when you don't
and free to
till you want
against rocks married to lichen,
ignored by otters juggling stones
smooth as distaste
a puffin hatching beside
a compass soaked with hurricane

II
The Girl in the Peapod

Tsuru no Ongaeshi

—based on a Japanese Folktale

Oui
mon amour,
I'm afraid

>if I knock on your
>door when
>you are hidden
>to the world,
>weaving silken
>brocades,
>selling them
>for the price
>>of being in love,

>if I knock on your
>door when
>you are bearing
>the frost
>for the future,
>eating a humble
>bowl of rice,
>vegetables
>>and disquiet,

You too will turn back
into a crane, fly away
never to return

Movie Date

We glide into the fly-in *NASA blanca*—
our antiquated pod rustling like pirated music

The usher, in his tablet, notes we'd like
to watch the movie + kiss (a word

our two moons situate on the opposite
spectrum of eucharist)

should I put you down for 50/50?
(in a rural asteroid dialect)

More like 10/90, I tell him, as you giggle,
spilling the pluto popcorn ©

on a stretch of unpaved Martian ground
With a straight face: *why don't you just*

make it 0/100?; his colleagues
snigger. We park our pod in the most

inconspicuous spot. *Ce n'est pas assez
caché,* you grumble. This movie set

on Earth: a staircase near a bombed-out
café where the heroine utters the same words.

The couple returns in a land-rover
scooter sputtering through lanes shaded

by real trees, negotiating roads fed
to grenades; he squeezes his legs against

her knees, grabs her thin waist till it breaks
four purple signals: *pourquoi*

ne me touches-tu jamais comme ça?
Tout est possible dans un film, mon chou,

et nous avons déjà beaucoup payé pour
   nos bisous. Ici, l'oxygène coûte cher,

ma chérie… donc, il faut que nous
   nous satisfaision de l'amuse bouche.

When you Travel

Clock-hands whirr
   like wind-vanes
before a hurricane.
   Having no time
for sleep or brunch,
   you drop
fountains, jugglers,
& tulips
down your surprise,
   tuck Montpellier
in your blouse.
But on your body,
my hands become
the traveller you are:
   insomniac,
       drunk,
              bones
delirious
       in a time-lapse
video under the skin,
seeking fireflies
& thrill till being sucked
out the train window.

Sketch of you reading my favourite childhood book

The quilt revealing your calves, ankles
entangled and swaying. Your spine—
its Soviet bent, published
in a Moscow before perestroika.
From my arm-chair, with French
      windows opened to the chill,
horses below the damned
      hills drawing spectral troikas.
It's strange for a man who scribbles
      to try to sketch you on the bed:
in the last page of a notebook meant
for you to copy my sole talent;
      now aimed at your afterglow—
  only fractured by your time
  to go.

Watercolour

We may soon not remember

If:

My dragonfly,
its black-
spine and yellow eyes,
              or the wild grass
sprouting
      from your belly-button;
—a just-kissed mole, this
neolithic art on the cave
   of your abdomen,
       envying the passion
in my kitsch—
were painted first

Or,

The ladybug near my chest;
the brush in your hand,
dipping into pastels
black   white   red
your half-buttoned dress…
over

teeth-marks, sweat,
and the gravity of doubt
endowing its every dot
with a fear strong enough
to event-horizon
this moment from our retinas.

Then,

Our first bath washed
it all—wings, smushed
compound eyes,
salt, scratches, camouflage
and tales: a dragonfly,
against ~~dravidian~~ Darwinian
odds, mating
      with a ladybug;
two children under a shower
taking turns shampooing
backs till they're still scented
with each other, and apple.

Loving your Poem

Since you didn't
orgasm,
you climax in your
poem: the first
of many you will write,
late into the night,
in Unicorn
pyjamas,
      in-
           sin-
                uating
a devil.

I see it clawing
through a moleskin
notebook till you rip
off its horn, carve
with its sharp end
the feelings
you never knew you
harboured.

I see you curled on
its cover, thumb-sized,
circled

by pizza crumbs,
yellow petals,
oily misses.
Stanzas—lilting
your head,
        a pair of childhood
earrings strung
on a tune delirious,
              demonic,

as you're telling
the cairns:
But I almost came.

Publishing

In you,

O editor

of the most revered

magazine,

thank you for accepting

this poem—

Its white font,

spilling out the margins,

wiped with the pink

eraser of my tongue.

My lines have never

been more fluid,

never reached so far,

like talismans

sold-out in the remotest

villages mourning

missing boats.

Editing You

Sous les bisous,
much as I try to never repeat
When?,
    Him,
        or Him,
I still do it, paranoid about
Us changing
to ~~Us~~.

The poets I edit tell
me I seldom force
them to erase their lines,
I listen
to their justifications,
then keep
them: senti-
mental sugar-gliders,
abandoned to philosophy—
That to accept the changes
or not, is
finally their pre-
        ro-
        gative.

But every
>   once
>   in a ~~whale~~ while,
a poem
withdrawn:
I cannot agree to these
edits, they change
>   *the meaning.*

Now re-inhabiting that memory,
terrorised
by the selfishness of wanting
to publish you in me,

edited.

Burning Question

After the teas,
      a harangue on smoking,
passive and not,
      or how some pretend
to take false-puffs,
      merely hold a drink,
to give others company…

Walking back
to our vehicles in pairs,
      you suddenly turn
around in mischief and whisper:
do you
enjoy it—the post-coital
cigarette?

Molly

'then he asked me would I yes to say yes'[1]

Just to say
she's well underway:
   all the moles in place,
      mood-swings
attuned to an atomic clock
   fabricated
from your most recent DNA
   (fished from the pocket
of a tweed-coat from
   the Outer Hebrides),
menstrual cycles.

I have christened her Molly,
   inspired
by *Ulysses*—wiring each hour
   of our feverish months
into a single day
   : every moment
on that bench, desire
   dropped in peak-traffic,
then picked up in areas

---

[1] *Ulysses*, James Joyce.

meant for rescue from a building
   belching hellfire.

All our firsts:
   including the inverted kiss—
you corrected the prefix in its
   sobriquet, not bat
before the man, but spider.
On circuit-boards intricate
   with webs after torrential rains,
I solder such marvels.
Buttons to unbutton the scented
blouse of your silences.

While you are in airplane mode,
I'm alone in an archipelago's
entrepôt, finishing Molly's soul.
I punch every poem into
a card, feed it while
my heart window-shops in purgatory
for frangipani and a crab-dress
whose haberdashery will remember
   my knees, palms, just outside
my library where it's made to wait,
               the sacred promise.

Can't

Because a caterpillar
chose my neck—
pink itchy blotches—still gnaws;
where once frangipani,
now bristling quiet.

Because apologies
are allergic, and the leaf
is munched by two stripping
fears, two sharks ambushing
a sick sperm whale.

Because sorry can't.
Because the cruellest isn't 'No'
but 'Enough'.
The skein in the ornithologist's
binocs, these cinquains migrating.

The Girl in the Peapod

It terrified us,
your stumbling upon
a photograph
where you are in a green
fancy-dress,
tailored like a pod,
giant toy peas lining
your ~three feet,
expressionless.
This kid, now an adult,
concealed in an
eponymous sobriquet
I dedicate poems to;
who knew?

My Glasses are Foggy Again

Since you can't clean
them for me,

I choose not to see the world
clearly, to keep driving

in this thunderstorm
without turning on wipers,

to race through
the miserable apparition

standing in the middle
of waiting and impatience—

adding frost to the number
on the speedometer:

now, a measure of temperature
inversely proportional

to our distance
If the warming is global,

why these growing icebergs
bearing your features?

Of an Alien Moon

Twilight already: the geese
follow you to a bridge
where lovers commit suicide
for sometime.
You know I wait for you
yesterday, today, tomorrow...
that you might bend my ear,
and whisper names
and temperaments
of all shooting stars
that have outnumbered
your counting fingers.

It's already late, even if
most of your basket
contains mushrooms
that have rained.
My hickey on your neck
is ready to hibernate.
I wait for you at the corner
of a nest with eggs
sheltering our twins.
Under planetary rings,
our lips are trapped
in a mammalian dream.

Accro

Néanmoins,
i
desire; peut-être
hopeless, St-
ill

Now
i
dwell
heartbroken
in

accro

Bless *St. Ill*

The Golden Aureole

Feynman's father taught him
to watch birds,
that names reveal little
about them.

This morning, you showed
me a Golden Aureole,
how it brings luck to have
seen one.

Barely a month before,
under the same tree,
a purse on the wall above
the bench, with 500 rupees.

That day we let the money be.
Today I learnt the name
of a bird so esoteric, then
just watched you

trying to spot *her* again.
You corrected me: *the males
of any species are more striking.*
I quietly let the misconception be.

*I wear yellow when I'm feeling
low.* Since I cannot be
of cloth nor feather, since my skin
is dark chocolate (your favourite),

given my lifelong immunity
to jaundice—I should stop gifting
you new books,
hound pages of elderly tree-rings;

picked not for their names
but so they flutter in your hands,
an interruption of golden wings
whenever you sneak inside the cage

of yourself.

Hff

L'indifférence dissout le langage, brouille les signes. - Georges Perec

Uff, umm, err, heh, hiss, tch, hmm—
but never heard hff until.

i
n
d
i
        a

Because I do not hope to Turing again...

But on the Loch Ness, drinking beer
with Spaniards,

far from Home (ffH).

Striking out the first letter of my first name;
the last letter of my nation's,

And ask:

Hff you love me, add
        Femme-Fatale's titular ancestor

till I'm left with an
>   an-
agram—
no, two: the official language
of the nation I was referring
>   to,

and the name I kiss
into—
Hff and puff till I blow
your house

i
n

I don't do gifts

Not
that I won't admit you're one—
how I'm altitudi-
nal near you, the mountaineer.
Just a benevolent whisper
and an avalanche burying everything
dead in me.

Rub this then,
every letter and punctuation
igniting the genie gifting
you a toy-train, a label stating:
this is not a toy, only
      a carriage of hardworking-coals
         moving your dreams

with its *chuk chuk chuk*,
beyond the Deccan to uncharted
terrains—iced fjords and bonfire—
tales pre-historic nurturing every
bite, lick and neanderthal voltage
you've missed
              through sacrifice, fear.

Not saying your patronus is
a dragonfly—I merely author
 personas, djinns,
antiquated trains that I hope
will romance against
your electric quarantines,
the nihilism you saw

in Dali's *The Persistence of Memory*.
When a melting clock
will blanket us,
 when I'll attempt
another sketch of you pronouncing
the (French) alphabet backwards
in your sleep.

Confessing in the Library

You might, finally,
one evening after card games
and drinks,
say it in a language
the *other* won't understand—
forgetting just the tone
is enough, and eyes
reveal too much
in a fraction of the time
the secret moves
        to the next page.
So he says it to her
in his library, as authors
wake their protagonists
up on the right-sides
of shelves,
and the poets too, envying
how they could never
invent anyone this foolish,
utterly lacking
in discretion for the love
of a woman who'll
never stop watching
from the spines

of books while he's trying
to write about her,
alone.

T minus N

'*Does it explain this interest in astronomy? Your having lived in the Lone Star State?*'

After all: Houston, Apollo 13…
The only trip, an insufferable
 ride with other students
from Beaumont, their Telugu
jokes in the bus, (paid
for the by the state of Texas)
      a Bangalore boy and girl
already in heat *fresh-off-the-boat*.
My Gujarati seat-mate and his one-
megapixel camera;
all travelling to a museum with asexual
simulations, the sole
astronauts-over-priced NASA teddies.
(something my cut-*surd* roomie
   would've molested in this land
of liberty)
All of us tourists: and to avoid
paying six bucks for the worst food
on earth, I feasted my eyes
on the tiffin-boxes of others; India
in every morsel.

*

I tell her astronomy is Mauna Kea
or Arecibo,
    that launches happen at the Kennedy
Space Centre in Orlando—Mama
and I escorted
by my aunt and her church friends:
a black lady,
        her daughter, who bought us
meteor ice-cream balls
        as I overheard her mother ask:
you've got that much money?
(hadn't yet read Rushdie, his *such-much!*)
Later, during a halt in the ride,
under an oak tree, a squirrel
thought me an extraterrestrial, nipped
me at T minus N.
First my passport, then visa.
A quick *Roswellian* search: '*squirrels
can't host rabies;*'. Then,
    red blood and Lufthansa: just *desi*,
not of Alpha Centauri, provoking
    a subtle, '*never return to our facility*'.

*

She is neither of Houston, nor Orlando,
(nor Baikonur). She's my launchpad
in cafés and class, near
father's garden and my empty bar,

always shuttling me into orbit,
at times from my car.
The real *nounours* aren't sold to tourists
craving images beside defunct rockets.
Exploration isn't
necessarily bound by the laws
of physicists or *ILS*. But
N, its two syllables, each taking turns
to receive and pump—
my ventricular pressure,
knowing sometimes I can make her sprint
like she's on the moon, 1/6th
higher—in our car, its console
and window overlooking
a stranger obscured by scarves,
that bird's cries she almost identified.
A kiss, and some—when did
the ~~counting~~ conjugating stop?

The car, a refuge against
the radioactivity of earthlings
      judging our velocity.
We, who are the atoms of an average
galaxy, with one black hole
at its centre, and the squatting stranger
who exits our sight,
our intimacy— fearing plague, or just being
polite.

Standard Candle

kismet/ co-incidence / intuition:
I should stop trying to label how I located

you from my (toad) nebula of sadness
I should stop feeling awkward

in role-reversing the fairytale here—my 3rd std
English teacher, Ms.Mercy, has underlined

kiss in red- her marginalia asks if nebulas
can kiss? if that's ink on my shirt pocket

or ... if I meant *frog?*—and,
I should resist the temptation to turn
quantum entanglement into

love by the sea (Ms.Mercy would mark
it in red)

        equations,
                like pecan pie, can crumble
        when there's an excess of event horizon or...

      ink
all this to say my love, my marsupial,
      I was mistaken your poems lack a narrative arc

[your pond of croak-croak-croaks
      deserves an imaginary font]

Get a Room

> *'There's sort of some weird sanctity applied to places.'*
> – Abbas

Sorry, not
where rancour is
more sanctified than affection,
        a hug,
    an intertwining of tobacco-stained
fingers with frangipani doigts,
a fingernail, its clandestine train
    tracing my shirt-back, lemon-tea
in one hand.
  A parabolic stroke on
a sub-rosa cheek,
  its shrapnel imploding
for weeks as souls pile till
    screams won't reach
  the tallest darkness.
Our public proclamations
antithetical
    to their education:
*How to Master a Language
  without Love—*
or write 283 mots
  about *amour* in Paris,

382 sanctities
    shackling *amour* in Pune.
My voting ink proves
    you argue without thinking:
The voter fingering a patriot
    in her respectable room,
climaxing to the O in
        Democracy—*my*
advice, you see…!
Sorry, I prefer
    aazadi,
I'll learn
  my grammar watching
  her angle her neck, slant her
pen, lick her lips
at the edge of my indi-
scipline.
I'll conjugate her
without shame, in spaces
    pedagogic made unsafe.
Not till there is a room, every bookshelf
  resisting the alliance of morals,
every vase with tournesols
facing a rogue star whose light burns us,
    in us
every window—
  overlooking a hearse

with a body like a princess's,
who abandoned 775 rooms in
the Buckingham Palace.

Will You Be There

Jackson Concert, Bombay, 2020

After you deleted
wish you were my first
—seeing
my passport photograph—
the only one
of four
      that says 'Bombay',
next to place of birth,
I thought I'd reveal
the truth: that though
I suck at parallel parking,
   I have visas
to universes parallel.

Can't remember
   how I came to you
   in the queue, asked
      if you have an extra-
ticket—you lol'ed
   with your friends:
      why not two?
this stranger with his

Old Monk breath, begging;
   until I showed you
the photo you still haven't
given me, of *the girl in
the peapod*, the poems
I have been dedicating
to.

Once inside,
I swear I was the only one
not mesmerised
by the moonwalking M,
and I only knew your name
began with N
when He chose to hug you
on stage—during
Will You Be There,
   that whale
soundtrack I still listen
to 7-ish-AM,
driving for you, then
the sea
too,
remembering our first
kiss—not sure why you
chose my lips when
everyone in the tumult
sought to rip the legend

off you, where probabilities
screamed
around the silence
 of us being our firsts.

Envelop

14 February, 2020

*Seulement mon
prénom—*
its letters never
cursive, creating spaces
you inhabit,
yet closing-in
like a shameplant's
leaves when your tongue
utters my two syllables.

But looking
at the j's
closed loop,
its area
expo-nen-
tiated
to n
where n is:

        nocturne
                nebula
        numinous
                nachtmusik

nounours...

or
just n.

To Salt

Let's begin with Gandhi's march to Dandi:
    only demanding from the sea
that it freely bequeath to its children

their NaCl, denied by
    colonial apathy.

*

The manuscript I sent
N—curated
with poems '*For the Girl in
the Peapod*'.

Her *St. Mah-Reese* response,
referencing King Lear:

'*I love it like salt,*

*how it's
wrecking my self-defences
    of Ambuja cement.*'

*

The mother's side of my family burns
its dead, while my father's

buries (till there was no land
to harvest bodies).

My great-grandmother, *Kamakshi,*
who'd chase me in nothing

but a white cloth, covering her
up to the 80-year-old skin under

her *Rudraksha* beads— because
I was young, and got away with undoing
her post-prayer hair-bun.
That night in the cemetery, her body
in the pit, doused with rose water,
lit by the penumbra of hurricane lamps,
then powdered
with salt.

After, we lay on the terrace
teary-eyed, trying to find her travelling

between the stars;
becoming a satellite revolving
around my cratered thoughts.

*

You asked if it was right, the sodium
chloride in your hummus—

I couldn't tell till after three days
in the fridge.
Licked

the bowl clean, before dipping
corn-samosas
while reading a *conte*
about a destitute brother, lending

his magic-mill to the richer who knew
there was nothing more profitable

                      than *sel*.

Alone in a boat,
he put the mill to task, might have become
the wealthiest man in the Caucasus
if only he knew how

to will it to stop—and that's how
grandmas still explain where

the sea gets its salt.

Insecurity

Behind the shell bookmark,
a quote from the *Sabato*
I lent you, the way it encapsulated
the three days on the beach
you spent
just thinking of me.

We're on the couch, not undressed,
and you unlock
your phone using my initials,
this slim device
holding your deepest secrets—
a slap on my insecurity's face.

III
Were It Not For

Not You

That awkward moment when you realise
the person in the distance is smiling
and gesturing for someone behind you,

and you wish

you hadn't reciprocated to this stranger
you thought you'd failed to recognise

How can you tell the world is not smiling
at you until it is too late,
and you are marooned by others' friendships?

Ice Storm

– Springfield, 2006

All night, the freezing rain.
I hear it string crystals on telephone wires till they snap like
    the necks of two negroes lynched in 1906.
Winter's apprentices blowing glass into firethorn berries.

Meteorologists claim such icicles form when a witch/[2]
zhalmawiz kempir,
    awakens from dogwood. That icicles aren't necessarily rockets
fleeing the afterlife's gravitation.

Within snowflakes, ladybirds tighten their scarves. Their cigarettes
fog my breath with the smouldering backs of horsemen.

---

[2] Ukrainian Witch.

Disgrace

The eponymous novel, with the dog on the cover,
poised to be something indefatigably

wretched—the first, or maybe
the only book you lent me; you said it was

a gift from your best friend, the one
who, you told me, smoked Günter Grass.

How things changed: soon, she wasn't
your friend anymore, and your library cozied

in with mine, into the shelf the church
gave us; we stood it next to the window

half-buried in dried autumn leaves.
It almost overlooked the veteran (Korea? Vietnam?)

scrounging for pennies near the tornado siren.
How all we had now seems dissolved in him, every dream,

forced into a stoop just so the emptiness may be pocked
with dirty minuscules that resist coming unstuck.

Don't Ring the Doorbell

The lady below us nursing her sickly hound
has her lights on all night. Like a daughter emotionally
bankrupted by her father, she props his furless underside
with her hands till he can pee on roses with dignity.

I picture her rubbing salve over his tumours,
half-attuned to the wine in our voices: me, reading
a poet you don't care for. That you're from his city offers you
the certainty of him having bedded his sister-in-law.

If you're right, I know exactly what he meant
when he wrote: *by narrow domestic walls.*
The lady below us who will not leave through her door.
Who must forgive the glare just so her dog

will not awaken to the nightmare that's its own body.

Carousel

Leukaemia, the necromancer, stole a kid
from my neighbours' life; the only night I slept

at their house, she traced
her teenage fingers upon my cheek, begged

me to find her at the carousel.
I push a skeleton off of a horse, take its place.

Invisible hands turn on music boxes behind my ears.
She's on the pony to my left; we take

turns going up/down. The boy from my school who
drowned with his brother—they share

a stallion. Corndogs. Every horse goes up
       as mine   goes down

The air   is   scented
 with cotton candy, sparklers, millipedes.

I even spot the little white mouse I choked
on my balcony (eyes fading out like infatuation)

Who is missing?   Who is?   Who?

Father of the servant girl I called an orphan;
He's lying between the horses, wasted on country liquor.

Ferris Wheel

On the ferris wheel, a girl holding her sister's hand.
She had it sawed off at the morgue
this morning. Her gaze is angled skywards,
where the clear night permits her Orion.
Like me, she enjoys being up here, however fleeting
the zenith. With her sis's hand, the girl pats
the head on my lap. I don't know who it belongs to.
This isn't altruism. My therapist said I should
have more fun, and I'm doing just that.
I avoid sitting in the toy train, beside mothers
clutching their still-borns. One time, I held onto
a Siberian Husky on the ferris wheel, counting
its last breaths. Counting can be prayer.

Park Train

A sign warning passengers not to feed monkeys
Still, an umbilical cord
(or more) disappears into branches

Red arrows blinking on the carriage floor indicate
the presence of an incinerator below

Whenever a body is dropped down the hatch,
a trill punctuates the sizzling; monkeys salivate

The engine doesn't resemble Thomas,
yet, we chant:

bless, you Thomas
from all of us, mommas

And only I mutter:

praise our commas

Will I be forgiven for not feeding you to the flames?
For riding interminably on this Park Train while
the monkeys hope?

Appointment

Mumbai, August 31, 2017

Just as I begin with the psychiatrist,
he has to leave.
No, I hadn't been following the news,
his friend all over the media, and now in a crematorium,
two days after the flooding,
        the manhole eight minutes from home—
  and open like a relationship
between justice and the world:
  be it a refugee child
washed up on foreign shores,
     or the doctor whose funeral needs my shrink
more than the burial I deny my feelings.

ELISA[3]

Kunchok Kyab crossed over
from Lhasa to Dharamshala,
screwing unprotected.

Of these yak-girls, the Dalai Lama
had no clue. Nor did this English dude,
who in his childless marriage,

adopted the Tibetan
lad who'd made a fool of the Chinese,
assuring him a monthly allowance,

rooting him in the temperate West:
our coding-hub in Pune so he
could thaw, maybe even matriculate.

As his only comrade, I barely remember
his anecdotes—mostly snow, bayonets,
and Himalayan typos (he keyed on

my father's *486)*, of a refugee anointing
himself in bowls of blood so the Buddha
       would realise the Buddha was dead.

---

[3] A preliminary blood test to detect anti-bodies reacting to the HIV virus.

Then his uncle, perishing in a letter
        from the home he could only
return to in memories unvaccinated.

Soon, a doctor said he couldn't explain
Kyab's weight loss. All night,
the mysterious smile of the Mona-

ELISA tormenting him, how
the People's Liberation Army had
invaded his immunity, would

shanghai his melancholic
songs flowing down the Deccan hills
in a language that could lose yet another

speaker, through a blood test, its needle
    drawing a sample
        in a clinic

near urinated walls kitschy
        with Safe Sex and AIDS,
located in a decade before drug-cocktails.

Mirza

His name has surfaced over the years, in taunts about
my father's communist leanings, in relatives' matter of fact

tones, proving to me he really did exist, this Mirza,
my father's comrade, lost to cancer before

I was born and how, decades later, his widow sweeping
the streets of Bombay is still sent father's money—not much,

never enough to support her children, but perhaps the only
atheist way he knows of keeping them in his prayers

Were It Not For

Historians will forget the fishermen, their 5000 boats and black
    flags. The dimensions
of the monument to the medieval warrior king is 210 metres
    tall and costs

enough to fund a decade of suicides for the state's indebted
    farmers—
having battled pests all their lives, it's natural they should end
    theirs with pesticide.

A feat like David Copperfield's, who in 1983, vanished
the Statue of Liberty to assert the importance of freedom,
    graces the inauguration.

The Hon'ble Prime Minister closes his eyes, rubs his temples,
    and the ginormous
monument of the maharajah brandishing his sword, disappears
    like the values

of currency notes. Indian pilots, flying Sukhois above the
    Arabian Sea, past
the kingless horse—to reinforce the disappearance, touch
    spectators' raw nerves,

stir erasure into their blood. Any fisherman volunteering to
    cast his net only hauls in
cow bones. The Hon'ble PM rubs his temples harder, and
    everyone is

in 1659, witnessing a grainy scene of a tiger-claw (بَگھ نَکھ)
    plunging into Afzal Khan's
chest. The PM opens his eyes. The maharajah is back on his
    steed, 420 metres tall.

The sea feels bountifully Hindu again. Gifts Bombay Ducks
    and shrimps
to the fishermen. A sword brandished at the sky, in case it
    starts raining Mughals.

Santa Clara

No matter where I go, I can't
figure out things by myself,
be it a laundromat, a poet's tomb,
or a ticketing machine;
like the one at Santa Clara station which
turned my anguish into tariff…

If she'd waited with my suitcase,
the walk to the train museum on the other
platform might not have seemed
as if I were dragging
my conscience just to buy some water

If she'd waited
with me for the train to Sacramento,
I may not have boarded the train
to Sacramento,
flown out the next morning
with a friend—he to meet his fading father,
and I, to schedule
my forgetting

Sacramento

Alaska Airlines has closed the gate.
We are late by ten minutes.
    Stranded with us is another family—
        the women are in hijab.
We learn their destination is Palestine,
        via Jordan. My friend's
            destination is a hospice.
The Caucasian lady doesn't register
our panic. Or offer regret.
Her demeanour turns us into ravens
vanquished by an infinite field of snow.
        The airplane is still on the ground—
it reminds me of a photograph, where
        passengers appear suspended above
a coffin wrapped in the American flag.
In this morning fragrant with bagels
        and Columbia grinds, we, who are
no martyrs, must find another way home.

Dubai

Every half hour,
        the smoking lounge;
His dad's cancer, too late for chemo.

Air-hostesses cloud around us;
here, they
        don't give a fuck
if our meal preferences are kosher or Hindu,
if seat belts can do kinky,
if aviation protocols gainsay universes
where our griefs are in-flight movies rated M,

one starring a man with a four day stubble,
blowing his smoke into
the netherworld,
& another who's unsure of what
he's turned his back to.

We are laughing because
        education only prepared us
                with machine-language and *Fibonacci*

        now,
        we are compiled into defeat.

playing truant

Last day of absenteeism, father bakes a pie. I stare
into the oven's glass, see yeast and planetary rings.

The VCR's first Hitchcock. An embezzler hits the road
while my dog lies buried in the garden.

I called her *Laika*—as mother predicted, the name
killed her more than the trash she'd eaten.

What else could await a stray named after a tragedy
 in space? The bunny I disinterred all week: Grandma

emptied a phenol bottle each time I dug up the mound.
I take father's pie to the pet cemetery, promise to dress

them in gowns. The lemon tree is still their godmother:
I situate its leaves next

        to stamps marked NOYTA CCCP.

My old man's photograph on Sartre's tomb

Cimetière du Montparnasse, 2014

Not about you *and* him
on the slab: mostly *TGV* tickets, gum, orchids and cigarettes

your passport photo in my wallet, that's felt turbulence, the tail of a milk snake,
and heard condolences offered from the lawn
to a queer home decorated
with Navajo art—parrots parroting the dog's
mournings for *Aurora*

Been through:

> *Vegas,*
> *New Orleans,*
> *Gotham,*
> *Coimbatore*
>
> Not Lagos nor Laos,
> Not Belize nor Sana'a,
> Not Tallinn (your first foreign trip;
>   the snow raising eyebrows at

>your Dravidian accent;
>your hotel: *Stroomi*,
>a pig said
>it sounds like *screw me*)

But maybe near the Oort
cloud precipitating courtship-closures, your
studio-mug left paternal traces

>*Chicago,*
>*Corpus Christi ,*
>*Bombay,*
>*Kolkata,*
>*Amsterdam* (from my pocket, you're listening
>   to my kosher stomach in
>   the hide-out of Anne Frank)

>*Paris.*
>*Paris…*

A wallet pressed against pole-dancer's
thighs, against Halloween throngs,
was frosted in -16° F,

remained stoic
that mild Missouri evening when the Toyota crashed
through two metal
barriers, stopping seconds away

from the sixteen wheeler
(your photograph refused to be crushed
in the impact)

Sometimes, it dropped whenever
I drew out a bill to pay for the addiction
you quit after 36 years,
when your legs
flared up in blotches
and you left
the dermatologist's office; held
mother's hand with meaning, really meaning

> *I*
>
>   *am*
>
>   *sorry*

Since I never hope to see your enlarged
b/w photo on a wall near the painting
of a surrealist horse; garland, jasmine
   and incense sticks
to show visitors who'd like you remembered
(just until they fast-forget)
by your only kid, though I wish
paradise is:

Noyyal,
       childhood water-hole

beyond the sugarcane
fields, where
snakes poked
out their tenements to see
how well us townsfolk accepted
guavas from a granny
greeting aliens
who encountered
her river in a diesel
Ambassador

two remembered cowries: an eel bracing
 my cousin's
belly-button, and for the first time,
you seeing my pubescent hair:

...*Baner,*
    Colaba,
        Cochin (but not necessarily
            in
                that order)

with Misha and Ché, you teaching
him—the man who won a continent's heart—
how to *socialise* with her, how she'll avenge
his Bolivian assassins in your marxist hell:
dog-forbid,
just rationally rabid!

it made sense extempore
to root you in prank; humourless and framed
in two dimensions
on a tomb made of three,
and interred next to his partner
who, with him once in her hand,
loved freely—
the gesture in Montparnasse, situating in every
existential dimension,
magnifying every other space
you've felt, heard from the time
you measured it with your HMT watch,
and the gregorian, moon-burnt nausea…
till you stopped, wound horology
to the blooming in your garden,
the dates on your coins—
Misha awakening you post-dawn
       with her colloquial Tamil barks.

Postcard from Stirling

Blinded by the blizzard when I see you

on the other side of the stream,

in the same summer frock you first wore back home,

and heard me read to you alone: lemongrass and tears

See, I didn't need to bring you as luggage,

I locate you when you think of me, or don't,

waiting in abandoned stations

where you numb secretly—sans song or suitcase—

When your pillow can no more absorb silences

In the snowcapped birdhouse, I hear you

sigh from an egg, its periwinkle shell

I was sitting by myself in a church one afternoon,

observing the candles throw your shadow so intently

that the stained glass asked me to leave

In a century old house, your eyes look up from a vase

on a windowsill, through the years we haven't travelled

And inside the store displaying tweed bags

and Chinese gowns, I usher your absence

into a trial room, hoping Scottish mirrors reflect

longing's dimensions

Butterfly Calendar

Flying in and out of time,
        cyclical numerals in squares.
Gregorian orchards pour nectar into months.
The paper is glossy with eyed-wings, bank logos,
the vernacular.

This is the only oasis on the barren wall,
a harbour for the lizard flicking its tongue at the clock.
These calendrical creatures cannot escape out of the open window
to settle upon benches delirious with spring
or fleet over a scooter's broken mirror.

                They will never cocoon,
or compete against parasols under cherry blossom.
Their habitat is a prison of pollen germinating the future;
a solitary net stalking seconds across time's undergrowth.

Passport

After wading through much
bureaucracy, I was issued
my new passport today.

I'm not as thrilled as I
ought to be, now that our
parting has become inevitable.

You are my passport to happiness,
and I need you for travelling above
these clouds of depression.

I wish my face remains embossed
in the first page of your mind, a memory
to which your eyes will

always remain open.

How They Went

My grandmother finally shut her

eyes, her last year spent in coma,

sinking deeper everyday,

gradually releasing the impending

truth, as if feeding her daughters,

blowing on a hot spoon each time before

letting them sip from it.

My grandfather, with a lawyer's directness,

was quite the opposite, he quickly died

of a heart attack, while my grandmother

prepared his coffee—

Everything changed within seconds,

but his law-books are still there,

upright and thick-skinned.

Why aliens shun India

1. The erotic sculptures in Khajuraho temples gave 'em a complex about their sexual mettle
2. Distressed the ancients could travel faster than light-speed even without spliffing weed
3. Addiction to Indo-Pak cricket matches threatened to disrupt plans of inter-galactic conquest
4. The realisation that trying to understand Indian politics was like teaching a black hole about tax-benefits
5. Inability to comprehend how a cosmic-package-trip costs less than a wedding/lehenga outfit
6. The impossibility of manoeuvring saucers through the air-traffic of a zillion mythologies
7. The religious/caste/astrological barriers against copulating with extraterrestrial sojourners
8. Alien docs fear a spike in diabetes owing to grocers who barter change for candies
9. The inedible grief of crash-landing in a Bollywood script, after attaining nirvana through Stanley Kubrick

Delhi, Texas

When told to 'go to Pakistan', they deported the government
— Dr. Baba Yaga

Delhi,

a community in Texas, Population: 303,
with one parish,
      one cemetery

and a post-office that's been sleeping
since the Great Depression— has opened
      its arms to the PM and his O
(despite plans of a wall for Mex-
                              ico)

Delhi,

      where tumbleweeds cross abandoned
railroads leading to detention camps

The roadkills of armadillos gathered in protest
      have been regretted by the national cabinet
            & the oppn claims even if the rattlers
                  win, there aren't any

(cotton) gins

Delhi,

    with its only school, where windows lookout
        to oil-derricks, where yellowjackets
            that populate benches, are taught
                to trade hives for fences

Editing

Don't follow a *the* with a the
or a *The*, or a *the* with a *The* or…
to trash every *thy* and *thee*,
please never *'revert*
back to me'.

Or a sky with a sky—though
the first, an archipelago
azure, airplane-less;
the second, another sky,
      with funnel clouds readying
a tornado to brunch
homes of (the?) newlyweds.

Don't end lines with an *or* or *to*,
almost never an *it*,
even when:
we couldn't see it / when the coffins
were breathing.
Maybe okay with: *it /*
returns her beloved, the foghorn…

I assert,
all these edits being
(rather) subjective.

[to what, Dear Editor?
 : bliss, ain't,
  poetries,
clones: *can't
 understand how* I feel!!!
  fuck, God,
 ~~spondee~~,
   an-a-
  pest, *lostalgia,*
ellipses bleeding past Munch's *Scream*]

www.ingramcontent.com/pod-product-compliance
Lightning Source LLC
LaVergne TN
LVHW010338070526
838199LV00065B/5755